A Higher Purpose

Copyright © 2021 Javonte' Wright, A Higher Purpose

All rights reserved. No part of this publication may be reproduced, distributed, or transmitted in any form or by any means, including photocopying, recording, or other electronic or mechanical methods, without the prior written permission of the publisher, except in the case of brief quotations embodied in critical reviews and certain other noncommercial uses permitted by copyright law. For permission requests, write to the publisher, addressed "Attention: Permissions Coordinator," at the address below.

Contribution by Kiyanni Bryan, Write It Out Publishing LLC in the United States of America.

Author: Javonte' Wright
Illustrator: Jason Josiah
Editor: Tamira K. Butler-Likely
Editor: Katherine Young

ISBN: 978-1-7371761-8-39 Paperback
First Printing, 2021

Javonte' Wright
The Wright Encounter LLC
Chesapeake, VA 23321
thewrightencounter@gmail.com

A Higher Purpose

Written by
Javonte' Wright

Write It Out Publishing LLC

Dedication

This book is dedicated to my Great-Aunt Carolyn Newby and my late Great-Uncle Lee Newby.

Thank you for your support over the years. Thank you for never giving up on me. Thank you for always being there with so much encouragement and wisdom. Most of all, I thank you for loving me! I love you to life & I miss you so much Uncle Lee: may you continue to rest in His presence.

To my late grandmothers: Grandma Sandy, Cathy Mae, Nellie Mae, and Marion: I love you and miss you dearly. May you continue to rest in our Savior's Arms.

I also dedicate this book to my closest friends, family, and individuals who have truly been there for me in my life. I want to say "Thank you" to Sabrina Newby, Novaja Wright, Jordan Mitchell, Alexandra Gatlin-Cornick, Jade Bails, Dazjae Johnson, Joi "Bells" Flowers, Jada Smith and so many more whom I love dearly.

Thank you all for being pivotal & important people in my life.

Table of Contents

Dedication v

REJECTED 1

MOLESTED 9

SHATTERED 15

ARRESTED 19

MANIPULATED 29

FORGIVEN 37

HEALED 41

A Special Thanks 46

REJECTED

A two-year-old baby boy, left alone in crib, not fed or bathed, just sitting there waiting to be cared for, waiting for someone to hear his cry. That baby boy was me. On October 4,1997, a seventeen-year-old mother from a little town in the country called Surry gave birth to a baby boy. A teenager had given birth to a child while she was still one herself. For her to decide to even go forward and give birth was a true blessing because being aborted was the other option, especially for a mother who never wanted any boys. On this day, God saw fit to give her what she didn't want. I have often asked myself for many years why I was given to this man and woman as my sister was born a year earlier. In the first six months of my life, I lived with my mother.

My parents were not married. My father was pretty much a "rolling stone": wherever he laid his head was truly his home when he wasn't staying with my grandmother. Around three months old, I began staying with my aunt & uncle on the weekends. In my mother's home—if it can even be called that—I do not have the best memories. I remember rainy nights and my mother hollering and yelling from the abuse my father would inflict upon her. The reasons why I will probably never know. My father was a tough and rough dude. Not many would ever think to cross him, for it could have led them to their demise. Still to this day, he has so much anger and frustration in his heart from things he has experienced. I'm unsure of all of his experiences, but I know that my grandfather was pretty much absent his entire life as well. In return, I think he found ways he felt like were good coping mechanisms. Being around him as a child at this point in life was not a favorable thing for me or my siblings. There were numerous times when I stayed with my aunt on the weekends and she would get ready to take me back to my mom's or dads and I would run and hide in hopes of staying with them. I would even throw bad tantrums and cry, but I still had to go back to my living hell. It may have made sense to take me back to my parents since they created me, but they sure did not act like they loved me.

There were many times in my younger years where my mother's three children by my father would be neglected in some way: whether it was not being watched, bathed, or sometimes even being fed. I did not understand how parents could have children and completely neglect them in ways where the essential things for life weren't being satisfied.

There is one day in particular that was one of the most life-changing days for me. I was at my dad's house, which was my grandmother's house, and my cousin Sabrina, my Great-aunt's daughter, found me in the house in the crib all alone. I hadn't had a bath in God only knows how long, and I had not been feed. She was so upset and bothered by this discovery that she went to tell her mother, and exclaimed how ridiculous this was and that something needed to be done.

At this point in time, I was already staying with my aunt on the weekends and would do anything to keep from going home. After having conversations with my Uncle Lee, they decided that they would petition for custody. They were prepared for a battle… but a battle didn't arise. When my aunt asked my mother for custody, she said

"Okay," and signed the papers. No second thoughts about it. She didn't ask for visitation or anything else. The same thing happened with my father.

Some background on my aunt & uncle: they had previously raised three children of their own and a grandson as well. They would truly help anyone they could, even if they didn't have the means to do so. I honestly believe that this example is part of the reason why I have the heart and desire to be a philanthropist. Growing up in the early 2000's was definitely challenging for me because what was the common reality for other kids was not mine. Seeing so many others have at least one parent made me envy my peers. I wanted and desired that for myself so much.

I couldn't understand why my parents didn't want me, especially my mom. I saw many examples of "deadbeat fathers," but to see and know my mother didn't want me either, left me feeling self-blamed and rejected. Aside from that, my aunt and uncle were in their 60's raising a little boy in a time when nothing is really relatable for them. There was a lot of friction when it came to different situations I went through versus their knowledge and experience. I would see my friends' parents advocate for their children and defend them, while mine would say "Turn it over to God and pray."

My response most of the time would be, "What do you mean pray? Everything don't need prayer. Why can't you be like others and go fuss the other parties out?" Generally, I would be told a story from my aunt that she would tell to encourage me, trying to relate but to be honest, I didn't appreciate it at that time. It was honestly years later when those stories became living memoirs to help me each day.

In school, I was the kid who got along with everyone, but I was never good enough to be a part of major things like being a guest at parties, invited for gatherings, going on trips to places like Busch Gardens, going out to eat, or to even sit with others at school during lunch. These were all things that kids wanted to be a part of that seemed "cool." First facing rejection from my birth parents, now facing it in my everyday life took a toll. In the midst of it all, even bullying began to transpire. For many years, I was mocked because I was the church kid, and people made jokes because I was heavier than most, and I was picked on because of my peculiar personality.

Now I must correct this old saying that I learned in school and was always taught to say though I learned was one of the biggest lies that has ever been told: "Sticks and stones may break my bones, but words will never hurt me." I learned that WORDS have power. When God created us, He gave us a tongue, and the tongue has been proven to be the strongest muscle in the body. As a matter of fact, Life & Death are in the power of the tongue. What does that mean? It means that things that we speak out of our mouth can truly come to pass, and there is power in our mouth. If you choose to speak life, encouragement, and positive things, positive things will happen. If we choose to speak negativity and evil things out of our mouths, then it will produce fruit of that sort.

We must be careful of the way we use our tongue. The words we speak can really cause a serious effect on others, especially if we speak negatively. Words are powerful, and they can hurt someone just as much as they can encourage. Rejection from my parents, rejection from my peers, and then I faced rejection in other relationships. I felt like I was this horrible fat kid that nobody truly loved.

No matter what I did, I would always be this child that had no real mother and father, no real friends, and no one to love. Just an ugly kid who was alone in this world by himself. To this very day, I can truly say I've never had a real relationship like with dating or courting as some say. Having been rejected in so many other areas of life, I was ashamed and scared to "shoot my shot." I did not want to give anyone the opportunity to say no. I knew that if I didn't ask then I could never be rejected in that aspect.

On a scale of 1-10, my self-confidence was at a whopping negative one thousand. My aunt would tell me talk to Jesus, tell Him about how you feel, cast your cares on Him. I'd think to myself *That doesn't work*. I tried to talk to Jesus, but I didn't hear anything. He was not listening, and He was the one that had allowed all of these traumatic things to happen to me in the first place. It caused me to feel like God didn't care about me. Here I was singing every Sunday, giving God the praise when inside of me, there was so much turmoil, so much pain, sadness, and hurt. I was like wait: I know this isn't what God truly would want for me. I knew deep down inside that I didn't want to feel this way, so I had to examine myself. After careful consideration, I realized I never took time to really listen to God, never truly waiting and meditating in his presence. I would say what I wanted, but never attempted to build a relationship with Him.

It was until I realized these things that a change was able to take place. Often in life, we pray to God only when we need Him. We pray to Him asking for a thing, and we say "Amen." We never attempt to go deeper in Him and stronger in His word. His word is one of the key elements that will bring you through. Even with Him allowing me to go through the hurt and pain that I experienced, He was the one who never rejected me. He never let go of my hand. When everyone else was gone, God was there all the time. All the private tears I cried, and the Lord God was right there beside me. I never took time to say "Thank you." I learned in this process to truly be grateful for my great-aunt & great-uncle being there to fill in the gap. I didn't appreciate what they had to offer for my life; I just knew what I saw in the world and wanted that.

    I remember not too long ago how I had a very impactful mentoring session with a preacher & gospel artist named Pastor Kim Burrell. She brought out some very vital things to me. She said to me, "Javonté, I want you to know that God allowed you to be with your aunt & uncle for many reasons, but one in particular that you should be grateful is for the advancement that you were raised in. You are able to receive wisdom from people who have lived on Earth for a long time already—people who have gone through many tests and trials. Ones who can give you the wisdom and encouragement that would be most beneficial to your life." After that conversation, all I could do was cry. It allowed me to go back to the hurt and pain I felt from childhood. In that moment, I realized how I honestly got the best end of the stick.

    If my mother had decided she wanted to keep me and raise me, I truly believe that I wouldn't have had a life that would be better than now. I know that I would have wanted and longed for more than she would've been able to provide. I would have been stuck in that little town to this day, not knowing how to get out or what was next in life. I don't believe I would even know God, and I can't imagine a life not having been exposed to Him at such an early age. On the flip side, if my father had raised me, I believe I would have followed in his footsteps. I could have become a drug dealer, been in the streets, in prison or even worse—dead—due to the choices of his type of lifestyle. I learned to be grateful for everything: the good, bad, and the ugly. We have to realize that not all rejection is bad. While it may not feel good and it most definitely does hurt, in some cases, rejection is necessary for our lives. It may not seem like that while you are going through, but I am a living witness that God will bring you through it all.

I know we have all heard it many times that "Rejection is God's Protection," and that couldn't be any truer. Right now, let's take a moment to really examine the times that we faced rejection. I mean really think about it: whether it was family, a love interest, or even a job. Let's think about what it caused us to do and the feelings we felt in those moments. In some instances, it will increase a burn or fire to overcome and rise above. And in others, its effect has the ability to affect us in a way of decreasing who we feel like we are. In this moment, I speak to those feeling discouraged and blaming themselves for being rejected or abandoned. Together, we take back the access that rejection has taken in our lives without our permission. Know that God has been and will always be with you as long as you let Him in. Won't you just let Him in? Let God wrap His loving arms around you and comfort your heart.

Let the Lord God begin to strengthen your heart. He cares about you and for you. He is so sovereign and wants to carry you in moments like this. He wants to lift you up and bring you through all that has hurt you. Rejection. Know that it is a part of life and know it is needed to help shape you into your purpose.

A HIGHER PURPOSE

MOLESTED

As a young, loving, full of personality child, I was used for someone else's pleasure and experiments. Around five years old, I was living with my Aunt Carol and Uncle Lee. Our home was the gathering spot for almost all events: cookouts, birthday celebrations when they happened, and most definitely the spot for all holidays. Whether it was Easter, the 4th of July, Thanksgiving, Christmas, or just "Sunday," the day the Lord has made, was reason enough for my aunt to cook a giant feast for the family to enjoy. During this time, living in our home was my aunt, uncle, my aunt's grandson, and my younger baby cousin, who had just been born not long ago, and my aunt raised her as well. Around different holidays, many different family members would come over. I loved when family came over, but many times for years after the age of five, I preferred to be in a room alone playing video games, watching television, or just spending time with my best friend's family for whatever occasion. Often, family members would come in my room to check on me, bother me, or just peek in to be nosey; either way, I would stay to myself. For a long time, I didn't understand why I didn't want to be bothered by my family when it came to them coming over. I never traced it back to this time in life.

One time in particular, I was joined in my room by a family member, where I was watching television, minding my own business. I don't exactly remember how events came about, but I guess the individual was bored. This was around the time when they were probably going though different hormones and puberty because they were about eight years or so older than me. For whatever reason, they thought it would be fun to sexually play with me. This was a relative of the same sex. As a child, I remember doing the requested task, feeling very scared and conflicted. I knew it wasn't right, but I was told to never mention what happened or tell anyone about it. Fear of getting in trouble meant I was going to get beat. Aside from that, I wasn't sure how to really feel about the fact I had experienced an unwanted sexual encounter and understand how to ignore the fact that it happened. This was definitely a life-changing event. It only takes one time for someone to violate you in a way like that. I was forced to do things that I could never imagine—even down to urinating in my mouth. I won't go too much further into details of the events that occurred, but on this day, I was molested by a family member.

    This event altered my mental state in so many ways. I was very confused because at this point in my life, I had never seen nor understood two people of the same-sex doing things of this nature, yet alone with a family member. In my head, part of me really started to believe that it was okay and natural, but in the same sense I felt like someone had been taken from me. A part of me was now tainted in a way that I personally didn't know how to recover from. So many questions and concerns in my mind arose. *Why would they do this to me? What did I do to deserve this? Why didn't I stop it? God, I thought you loved me...* so many questions I just couldn't understand. So, what did I do next? I did like most victims of sexual abuse: I kept it to myself. I hid it deep down inside, trying to bury the things that transpired in my childhood. In the Black community, many things like sexual abuse are swept under the rug. If you confide in anyone, many times if they haven't been through it themselves, they will tell you to just pray and forgive. It is more to the healing process than just that when it comes to something of this nature. If you were anything like me full of hurt, rage, confusion, pain, and much anger came into your heart towards many different parties, especially your abuser. In my case, I had to continue to see this individual for years not knowing what to do, how to respond, or how to even interact with the person who took something from me that I couldn't get back. My purity and innocence had been taken away from me. For a long time, I blamed myself, but in all honesty, what was I supposed to do at such a young age? I didn't have the strength or power to physically move someone who was greater in size and strength than me. I didn't know to call for help or tell someone even when I was told not to. I didn't know who I could trust. I was upset and bound for so many years.

I hated this person who took away my innocence. I mean, I hated him, but I knew that I had to love him as well. I struggled with being able to move past all the trauma this person had caused, altering the way that I was created to be. It was until I grew up and really learned in church that the molestation and abuse were not okay. I knew how I felt, but to find out that it really wasn't an okay thing was just mentally mind-changing. I looked at men in a different way than I had before. I knew it wasn't right, but at the same time, I felt it was okay because of the premature exposure to sex and with it being with the same gender.

I didn't know who to confide in, and it felt like it was just me in a world of so much chaos and confusion. I knew that I wanted to be delivered from everything attached to this part of my life and the cycles that it created. I knew that I didn't want a generational curse to be birthed or carried over. I knew that the traumatic event had to break but "How?" was the point of struggle. I knew God could heal me, but I knew that work had to be done.

"Where was I supposed to start?" was the constant question I asked myself for fifteen years since the event. My pastor had preached many messages about forgiveness. One Sunday, he was talking about forgiving those who had hurt you. In hearing that, it finally hit me. Forgiveness was a thing that must be done in order for me to begin the healing process. Forgiveness needed to be given from me to my abuser, and I had to forgive the one who caused me to go in such a downward spiral for much of my childhood and teenage life. I had accepted that this was necessary and forgave this person. It was so much easier realizing it than doing it.

I had to go to a place in myself and ask God to help me to forgive, help me to see and feel the forgiveness for myself. I realized that what happened to me most likely wasn't the first encounter my abuser may have had. I took into consideration that it was possible that the very same thing or maybe something similar happened to them to cause them to even be interested in doing the same thing to me. I realized in the moment while forgiving that whether they took responsibility or not, they were still worthy of being forgiven. God has given us countless new mercies and His wonderful grace is for us all. No matter how bad or horrible a person is, God's grace is big and wide enough to cover each and every single person in this world. Who would I be to choose to not to forgive someone?

No matter how bad someone hurt you or wronged you, remember that God's grace is what saved you when you fell. His mercy is what spared you. He loves us all so much that even the worst thing that we have done, He chooses to grant us grace and mercy. Who are we that God would love us that much? We are everything to God. We are his children. Even in all of our faults, God still shows us His love by looking beyond all our sins and he doesn't forsake us. Instead, he forgives us and he cast it away to where even he won't remember it. That's the love that he has for us. We should have this love for people despite what they have done. I'm not saying don't forgive and forget, but I am saying allow God to take the pain, hurt, and turmoil away from those things that trigger you. To have been molested, raped, or experienced any type of sexual abuse is a challenge in and of itself. If you truly want to be free from those demons who haunt you from the past, turn everything over to God. Allow Him to come into your heart and mend all that has been shattered.

A HIGHER PURPOSE   14

SHATTERED

I was a shattered teenage boy trying to gather all the pieces of my life and find out who I was. After dealing with rejection and being molested, it left me very broken inside. The healing process took years. I found myself on a constant search for validation in everything I did. My past tore me apart on all sides. I didn't know how I was going to go on for much of my preteen and teenage life.

I wasn't a child who got into much trouble growing up in school, but I did sometimes at home due to the trauma of abandonment and the abuse had left me broken. I had a hard time following simple directions such as cleaning my room and being obedient. My mind has always been running at one thousand miles per second, but at this time of my life, I had so much chaos running around me that simple things didn't come easy to me. I would want to do the opposite no matter what was being asked of me. Growing up in Carolyn & Lee Newby's household, there was absolutely zero tolerance for behavior problems. That meant I was going to get my gluteus maximus tore up for what they deemed as disobedience and disrespectful behavior. They did not believe in "sparing the rod and spoiling the child." I knew not to act up outside of the household, but inside the home was my safe haven, so I didn't know how to receive it to be just that.

A major effect from me going through various challenges in life was my need to always be & feel defensive. If I felt in any way that someone was trying to attack me or challenge me in a condescending way, I would immediately be tapped in—and not tapped into Jesus.

All the hatred that was stored in my heart would be ready for anyone who was willing to step to me, even towards those whom I loved and cared for dearly such as my sweet, loving auntie. There was one time in particular that I was so triggered by something she said, and I lashed out with my words, which pierced her heart. I knew when I said what I said that it was wrong and hurtful. I didn't take into consideration of the effect that it would have on her. When she cried that day, it was something that I had never experienced. One of the strongest women I know in my life, her heart was broken due to words I used. This was a day when I learned to truly be careful with my words and even my thoughts. As stated before, our words have so much power.

Our thoughts precede our words, our words precede our actions, and our actions will precede consequences and results. The enemy will use a shattered-heart person to give you the ammunition that you may not even know that you possess. The lethal ability of the tongue is unprecedented, and it's until you have a moment where you feel attacked that its ability can be unleashed.

After this event, I immediately felt like I had just burned a whole in my heart. My auntie is my heart and I had just unleashed my wrath on her. All because I was broken and didn't know that I was too far gone. All I could do was apologize to my aunt. Thankfully, she is a true woman of God and forgiveness came like second nature for her, but it didn't remove the effect right away. Healing took time.

I went above and beyond to show my aunt that I loved her dearly and I would never allow my words to hurt her again. I was so upset with myself for allowing the enemy to use me in such a way. I couldn't believe how he had just crept in without my permission. Then again: was it really without my permission?

Allowing myself to be consumed by my pain and hurt was all he needed to attach himself to me. He knew that back in October 1997—the day I was born—he was going to have to do all he could to destroy me. He knew that God was going to use me as a vessel to be an advocate for Him. To help others identify him, cast him out, and break free from the bondage of the wilds of the devil.

In this brokenness, there was a boy whose confidence was below a deficit. My confidence was nonexistent at this point in my life, especially after the bullying that I had encountered. I felt as if I would never amount to anything. Some way or another, I felt like I was going to fall into my parents' path. I hated the way I looked, no matter what my aunt bought me to wear. I felt like I was never enough.

Torn apart from the inside-out, I honestly just wanted to give up. Compliments on occasions where I looked decent, on the inside, I truly felt like the ugliest, tallest, and fattest being in the room. I was so torn up inside that it was like a tornado had come into my mind, heart, and soul—wreaking havoc everywhere. It was like a constant never-ending hurricane, just cycling around and around. While the tornado and hurricane were spinning around shattering and breaking each other colliding and dividing but in the midst of the cyclone there was the eye of the storm, full of peace and hope. The potter of humankind was there in the middle of all the chaos just waiting for me to fall on my knees and say, "Oh Lord, Help Me."

Once again, I was in need of help, but never really took the time to cry out to God. I knew that it was timeout for any games. It was time to really seek the Lord. To really seek His face, to learn what it is to really have God on my side. To know that He would never forsake me was mind-blowing. I was truly a man after God's heart but I wasn't quite ready to let Him in mine. I made the choice to put my trust in Him.

I decided to allow Him to come in my heart and do a divine transforming of my mind. He spoke to the storm that was raging inside of me and said, "Peace Be Still." And it was still. See, when God speaks, even the storm has to obey. He wants to come in and mend up all the wounds. He wants to take all of the pieces and be the adhesive to bring them back together. He is more than able. God is so sovereign. He wants to be the molder of your life, but you have to let Him begin the work in you. No matter how fragile, sensitive, broken, or shattered your pieces are, if you allow God in, He will take you through the process and put you back together again. After He puts you back together, you will be able to take on the world. With God on your side, all things are possible: just trust Him.

ARRESTED

As a young man beginning to walk into my calling, I got into serious trouble. Back in primary school, I hated reading. I felt like it was not necessary and didn't really mean anything. It was until my first-grade teacher had a conversation with my aunt about holding me back another year because my reading wasn't strong. My aunt, like any good parent, told my teacher to do what was necessary for me to be successful, so that meant I had to do first-grade again. I was so embarrassed and humiliated to tell my friends. In all actuality, I was reading and writing at a middle school level mainly because I had an above normal vocabulary. I guess that came from being raised with older guardians who taught me a lot of the "older seasoned language." I just didn't think it was important and I told my aunt some years later and thanked her cause while I didn't like being held back and was upset for a moment, it was the best decision.

A few years later in sixth grade, I was performing above the average sixth grader, and my teachers knew about my story of me being held back. They felt I would be a good candidate for this program called PAL. This was a program in Chesapeake Public Schools that had been going on for some years. It was created for students who had been held back in previous grades before sixth grade and they would be able to come to a designated location and complete seventh and eighth grade in the same academic year. Students from all over the Chesapeake school districts would come to this program with generally two to six kids from each school. It was an extremely fast-paced program, but I felt like it was an honor and privilege to be recommended. My aunt was so happy and encouraged me to go forth, so I did.

I truly enjoyed the program and loved my two teachers. I really connected with my homeroom teacher. She was very kind and sweet until one day, things changed. Well, they seemed to change every other day. Three other classmates from my school, Western Branch, would sit with our homeroom teacher every day for lunch. During this time, she was able to learn as much about us as we learned about her. She told us how she suffered with a bipolar disorder, and in my head, I wondered if she went to counseling because it was necessary, but I never asked since I was the child and she was the teacher. I started noticing that some days, she really liked me and other days, she acted like she hated my guts. She began writing me up for the stupidest reasons—things that others weren't getting referrals for. I didn't turn my homework in once and she wrote me up. This was a time when I was definitely going through the hard parts of my healing process from rejections, molestation, and much more, which made me more defensive.

I never disrespected her, but I definitely questioned her decisions when it came to writing me up. She never once contacted my aunt about any of the problems she was writing me up for nor did the principal when I went to their office. It felt like everyone was working against me except the ISS (in-school suspension) teacher. She realized that something didn't make sense. She saw my true character and didn't understand why I kept ending up in ISS.

Prior to this, I hadn't been in any type of school trouble since elementary age. I wasn't one of those problem kids who always got into trouble. This cycle went on for a couple months, and I would tell my auntie that I just wanted to drop out and go back to regular seventh grade although she never knew about the unfair treatment I was receiving. She would just keep encouraging me and lifting me up and I kept thinking *This was too much*.

In this same year outside of school, I had the chance to sing in the state choir for the first time. I am a COGIC (Church of God in Christ) child and I grew up in the First Jurisdiction of Virginia where my bishop was the Late Great Bishop Ted Thomas Sr. (may he continue to rest in his presence). We had our annual Workers conference in Richmond and I would ride the church van every night to sing in the choir. I was one of the front-line singers. My pastor, my family, and church family were so proud that I stepped outside of my comfort zone and started to walk into my calling as far as the music ministry side. It goes without saying that the devil was mad about this happening, so he decided that he was going to use me in a way that was going to just destroy my life.

Literally, the very next week the temptation of the enemy fell into my lap and I walked into a door that I didn't even know I was opening. It was another day that I had gotten into "trouble" for something so benign. In my mind I was trying to figure out if this teacher really cared about me. I wanted to know if she really cared or just hated me. What was it about me that she only would pick on me and single me out? I made a plan to write a note and leave it in my chair. The first note I wrote said, "If I had a gun, I would shot J.W.," which are my initials. My grammar wasn't even right. In that moment, I heard a voice say "Nope, she won't care so much unless you put her initials." So, I changed the initials from mine to my teachers. I didn't think anything of it and I left the note in my seat.

I got on the bus and fussed about the teacher with my "friends" and went home. By the time I got home, my aunt had received a call. She immediately was hysterical and kept asking me, "What did you do?" I instantly broke down in tears because I knew I was in trouble. She said the school wanted to have a meeting with me the next day and I told my aunt what happened. She started to blame herself because I had previously come to her about this teacher, but I told her it wasn't her fault and I took responsibility. I had no idea what tomorrow was going to hold, so I just remained to myself and gathered my thoughts. I knew I had no intentions of harming anyone. To this day, I struggle to kill a bug yet alone a person. Not a bone in my body could do so. I decided to clean out my backpack, emptying all of the contents and washing it out. I don't know why I did that, but I felt led to do so. I often had food containers and silverware in my backpack from field trips and church trips with the choir.

The next morning, my aunt and I went the school and we had a "hearing." I was shocked and did not realize how serious this was; what had I gotten myself into? They let me know that it was illegal to write a note of such magnitude and it not be taken seriously. It was known as a threat and they let me know they would have to do a search. I agreed especially since I knew I had no intent to harm and I had cleaned my backpack. As they were nearing the end of the search, a butter knife falls out and my aunt and I both gasped. *Where the heck did it come from!* I absolutely had no idea where it came from. They recorded the hearing and I thought I was going to be able to leave with my aunt, but a police officer came in and let me know I would have to go into custody. The threat was a felony and having the butter knife was a misdemeanor. I had a "Color Purple" moment with my aunt and did not want to be separated from her. I had never been away from her since I was I toddler. I was so ashamed of myself and what embarrassment and pain I caused her.

From the school, I was enroute to Tidewater Detention Home or T.D.H., which was also equivalent to juvenile jail. My mind was all over the place. I didn't know what was going to happen to me next. I went through processing and booking. I felt so alone and cold: no way out, just trapped by my own doing. Section 6 were my living quarters, and all I knew to do was find a bible and pray. When I opened it up, the first thing I turned to was a passage about disobedience bringing God's judgment and I just cried my heart out. I cried out to God because I did not understand why this was happening to me. I knew that I hadn't always been obedient to my aunt and uncle like I was supposed to, so I accepted the consequences and asked God to forgive me.

I went down the line from everything in my past. I went to Him as humbly as I knew how. I had my first court date and my aunt and uncle had missed the first time but the judge said she would come back. By the grace of God, they made it and I had my legal hearing. This is when I learned how prosecutors lie. I mean they lie so bad, it's not funny. They made up lies about me looking for her address and trying to find her so I could go kill her. The judge asked me did I want a lawyer or to represent myself. At first, I was going to say myself but I heard a voice tell me ask for a lawyer, so I did. The prosecutor did not want to let me out of jail but the judge said granted me house arrest. I was so thankful to God; I may not be free but at least I could be with my family.

The only thing I asked for was to be able to go to church on Sunday and the court system granted that wish. After six days of being locked up, I was finally able to get out, and on my way out I saw the counselor who interviewed me when I went in. When she met me, she said, "There is something about you and that you don't belong in this place. It's not for people like you." As I was leaving, she let me know that she didn't ever want to see me in there again. I said, "Thank you so much and you don't have to worry about that."

Things looked to be turning in my favor until I went to my first meeting with my lawyer. She let me know I could be facing three to five years in jail for what I had done. My aunt and I both started crying. I couldn't imagine a day without her, yet alone five years. My lawyer asked me how I wanted to plead for the charges and I said, "Well, I did write the note, but not for the reasons the prosecutors posed and I honestly did not know that I had the butter knife." She helped me fix my statement with the correct words, and I pleaded guilty on one account and no contest for the other. The lawyer then informed me that we would prepare and she asked if I could get any letters that described my character? My aunt and I went to work requesting five letters. Everyone who knew me understood that none of what happened was my character. I knew that everything I was going through was so much bigger than just me.

On the flip side, I had to have another hearing with the school board and chairman. This was to determine if I was going to be expelled or sent to an alternative school. I knew my aunt was praying hard, but I had to tap in for myself. I didn't want to be kicked out of school forever. It was crazy how in just a few moments the enemy was able to use me and the effects could change me for a lifetime. After pleading my case to the board with my aunt, she became even more passionate and had my back more than ever. She spoke some amazing words and it softened the hearts of those in attendance. They decided it was best for me to go to alternative school and I needed to be there for a couple of years. I was filled with joy, excitement, as well as fear. I was scared of what was going to happen next, what kind of people who were in alternative school. I was scared of how I was going to be judged and treated. I had to get all of those thoughts out the way because the decision was effective immediately.

  Still with my house arrest bracelet on, I started to go to back to school. My class was very small, and I liked it for the most part. My teachers were able to give the extra attention, which was a plus because many students needed it. While I didn't need the attention, I did appreciate it. Here is the first testimony I failed to mention. I was in alternative school as an eighth grader, meaning that I was going to still be caught up in my right grade. They had the option to place me back in seventh, but because of the pace of PAL, I was way ahead of the regular eighth grade curriculum. There were two special teachers I had while in alternative school: Ms. Garnes, my history teacher, and Ms. Edwards. They were strong-minded Christian women who were very intricate in days to come at the alternative school.

  One day when I went into my history class, I could feel something different about the class. It felt very sad and gloomy which was not normal. I went over to Ms. Garnes and I let her know that I could feel a change in the atmosphere. The change I felt was death. This was the first time in my life I had ever felt anything and it had an effect on me where I had to say something. She looked at me in shock, confirming that she had lost her father. Immediately, I gave my condolences and consoled her. I thought nothing else of it. She and Ms. Edwards had been talking about me and they spoke on this event. Ms. Edwards sat me down one day at school and said "Javonté you have a gift and it's strong even at a young age." I sat there in amazement wondering what gift had displayed itself. I didn't remember singing at this point. She said "Discernment. You have a strong spirit of discernment."

Until that day, I don't think I had ever heard that word. Not in church or Sunday school, and if I did, I wasn't paying attention. It sparked interest so I went to research it and to my surprise, it was when I began to get answers for things I wondered over the course of my life. I never knew me sensing things good or bad was the Holy Spirit leading and guiding me. I thought about all of the times people would ask me things and I gave sound advice, and it wasn't really me like I mentioned before. This explained why many times I couldn't remember what I had said, only that it helped the selected parties. To me, that was a life-changing moment that I would not have had if I was in a regular school. I was there in alternative school to be an impact on the teachers as well as the other students. I started in late March and school ended in June.

Testimony number two: the principal of the alternative school named Mrs. Herbert called an all-student end of the year assembly. All parents, teachers, and students came. In that meeting she stated that "This has been a wonderful school year. There were some students who have come this year that I wish I could keep, but they just don't belong here. They belong back in regular school." Now I don't know how many others she was talking about, but I could feel in my spirit that I was one and I leaned over to my auntie and said, "She has to be talking about me." Just as sure as the sun rises in the morning, I received a letter from Chesapeake Public School district reinstating me to regular public school to attend as a ninth grader. Even in my wrongdoing and faults, God still showed His grace and mercy.

Now back on the legal side. I had been on house arrest for six months and it was time for my last court day. In the time leading up, I had received over 20 letters from pastors, neighbors, teachers, friends, and family who all wrote about my character. There were so many letters that really spoke the truth of who I was. Sometimes, I go back and read them and cry. There is so much hatred in the world and for someone to care enough to put something positive in the atmosphere about me is just mind blowing. I am forever grateful. We turned in the letters to my lawyer and she turned them over to the judge. My court date was scheduled around 10 AM, but for some reason, they hadn't called us in yet. I was scared and afraid of what was going to happen. At the same time, I knew that God didn't bring me this far to leave me. Finally, they called my name and we entered the courtroom.

Judge Olds called me up to the stand along with my aunt. She said, "I apologize for the delay. We were trying to get everything finalized. We have decided that ALL THE CHARGES WILL BE DISMISSED. You will NOT HAVE ANY CRIMINAL CHARGES. No felony nor misdemeanor. All I want you to do is sing." I was completely in shock and disbelief. Did she say 'Aall charges dropped? NO Record?

Did she just ask me to sing in the courthouse?' Yes, yes, and yes. My aunt stepped in and wanted to let them know I was hoarse from singing at church but the judge was like just give us a little bit. The first song that came to mind was a song from the state choir that really expressed the sentiments of my heart. The song says, "You are worthy of my praise, you're worthy of my praise, the ways you made for me… the doors you've opened for me… Lord, You're worthy of me praise." I sang that little bit and the prosecutor who was totally against me said, "Wow, if that's how you sound hoarse, I would love to hear you full voice." I was a free young man.

God allowed me to go through this for so many reasons. All of these reasons are tied to my purpose. I want to let you know that no matter what you are facing, if you give your life over to the Lord and allow Him to take control and be God, He will do just that. There is no situation or system He cannot infiltrate. He is the master of them all. God is the Ultimate Supreme Judge. God has the ability to wipe things clean as if they were never there. He moves like that for His children, those after His heart. Even when we mess up: if our heart is for God, He will pick you up. You can lean on Him, and He won't let you fall if you just lean on Him. Say you decided to not lean on Him, the Lord God will pick you up. He is the only one that will truly never forsake you. Trust in the Lord God, again I say Trust.

MANIPULATED

At any cost, I wanted to fit in with my peers. When God created me, he poured in me a huge box of empathy. In my opinion, this was truly a blessing and a curse. Being a lover of people and having the gift to connect with many, I did not realize how vulnerable I would be to manipulation. I would give my last to people—many of whom I did not know. There were some drawbacks to having a big heart due to the type of people (spirits) who were attracted to me. Have you ever heard of leeches and parasites? Uh-huh…these worms manifested themselves to me in the human form.

As I was building my relationship with God, I had accepted my calling as a young worship leader. I primarily sang at my home church and would accept some invitations at local churches. The enemy was very upset because I was using what God had given me to tear the devil's kingdom down in small but impactful ways. During this time, the Lord connected me with some people whom I thought would forever be in my life. I didn't want to lose them for anything. These people began to fill the void that I had for siblings. While I had eight siblings from my dad, my mother, and all the other mothers of my blood siblings, we didn't really have much of a relationship. One parent in particular hated everything that had to do with my father and sheltered her children, so she made sure to keep my siblings away. This made me long even more for close relationships.

Nevertheless, here I was so grateful for these people who I just knew that God sent into my life. How naïve of me to think that when the mindset of the people alone wasn't of God. I still just believe they were of Him.

These "friends" of mine were flocking around me, really felt to be so genuine when in actuality, they were only after what I was able to offer. Advice was the thing that everyone came to me for—especially relationship advice. Now if you remember from before, I had never had a real relationship. So here I was giving advice on topics I had never experienced, but somehow, I was able to share sound advice with others. I found out some time later that my "expertise" was called discernment. I really was just getting into a place where I was allowing God to use me; I didn't know that He would send lessons to teach me more about human nature. It was in this time where people would also come to me about their financial problems. They didn't always ask me straight up for money but they would prey on my empathetic heart. They would tell me their situation or problem and I felt it was my duty to help them.

There was one individual whom I'll call Stacia that I loved so much and was there for her every beckoning call. In fact, I went through two thousand dollars for Stacia in a month's time, just trying to be supportive in all that she had been going through. Then we had a falling out. I was devastated. I did not understand why God would allow everything to end the way it did. I had a conversation with this lady who has been a key spiritual advisor in my life since middle school and in the conversation, she brought out to me something that I had never considered. She said, "Javonté, when you are there for someone and are filling the need that they should be going to God about, you become their God. What would someone need God for if you were there to do His work?" I was speechless because I had never examined the situation and realized how I allowed someone to come and infiltrate my heart so much so that I became the thing they would come to when in need. I had to ask God to forgive me for stepping in the way and not following Him nor allowing Him to guide me.

While I truly cared for Stacia, I was no longer going to allow them to control me and use me for what wasn't meant for them. Aside from that, a few years later, I went through another cycle with this particular issue. This situation was different because it had taken me to a place where it seemed like I was so far from God; it felt like He stopped speaking to me. Over the years, God tested my ear for His voice. At a young age, He started to speak to me. In the beginning, it was through dreams and then it progressed to His voice. I want to take this moment to say if you are questioning whether God is speaking, you know that He will never speak anything to you that will tear you down or destroy you. When God speaks, it is either to bring light to different situations, encouragement, hope, help you to open your eyes, or convict the human soul. Know that if God chooses to speak to you, cherish it with your life! It is one of the most reassuring and beautiful experiences I have ever had and I will never allow the enemy to get so close where God will stop speaking to me again.

In the fall of this same year that I was helping others, I was connected to a different individual during a hurricane that was on its way. They needed help and my heart jumped to be of service. Instead of one day of help, it seemed like I began helping this individual every day. Suddenly, a death happened for them and everything changed. They had to now be responsible for not only themselves but a sibling as well, and needed transportation everywhere. Who better to help than Captain Javonté to the rescue? I began every day driving from my hometown Chesapeake, VA to Virginia Beach, sometimes two to three times a day to help this individual. I would often fall asleep behind the wheel and no one asked or cared about what I needed. When I would bring up my concerns, I would be told that I shouldn't feel that way or the sentiment would be "We need you—don't leave us." I was feeling myself drawing further and further away from God. This individual had some demonic entities attached to them from their past and they wanted me for all the wrong reasons.

They wanted me dead. I began having suicidal thoughts from overwhelm. I felt like I was too deep in this hole. I had nowhere to go or anyone to turn to. I started seeing a goat figure in my dreams, and next to me while I drove, as well as in the shadows of the night. I had seen and felt demons before, but never of this magnitude. This demon was after my life.

I was initially blinded in not seeing that it was connected to the individual. Old pains of the past began to resurface: old feelings began to wrap around my legs so tight that I was really beginning to feel and get tricked into thinking I was ready to end my life. Death by my hand seemed to be the only way out.

Over the course of a few months, I was living more on the beach in a motel with the needy individual and their sibling than I was at home. My aunt knew this was outside of my normal behavior, and she was very worried about me. I believe she knew that soon something was going to happen if I didn't get reconnected to the Light of all Lights. Her prayers are what saved me. I felt them pulling me to come home. I felt them calling my name. I had to do some research on this figure of the ram/goat beast that I kept seeing and feeling. I knew that it wasn't going to be good, so I was preparing myself. When I looked up the image that I kept seeing which appeared to be a goat man, I saw the demon I was seeing. In that moment, I really saw how it was tied to all that I had been doing—including fornication. Even though it was only once that is all it took, just like with children, it only takes one time for a woman to get pregnant. Let me set the record straight: I was never one to be messing around with a bunch of people like a hoe, but I did have the desire and appetite for it.

Stemming back to childhood, I wanted to see what was really going on as far as the s-e-x word and figure out how things went since I never had the "birds and the bees" conversation with my aunt and uncle. On the day before Thanksgiving, I had about ten orders for a special dish I make called carrot soufflé (yes, I am a chef in my own right). The individual had asked me to take them to a place and I informed them that I needed to go to the store at a certain time. They couldn't have cared less, and they literally had me waiting for an hour and a half. The last store had closed and I realized that I was seen as less than dirt to them. If it didn't benefit them, then it didn't matter. I had to cancel all my orders because I couldn't get what I needed and I was no longer joyful. I have to be in a good mood when I cook because it can truly be tasted in the outcome. It may seem small, but it was like when the events unfolded, it snapped me out of my trance where I was okay and accepting of this vicious cycle.

That night is when I really woke up in knowing that a change needed to happen, but how was the question. I felt like I was too far gone for God to even hear me. I went to my aunt because she has always been known to have the best advice and in this moment, I didn't know where else to go. I told her that I had messed up and didn't know what do. I opened up to her about everything I was going through and told her about the demon that was trying to attach itself to me to kill me. I had gotten to the point where I just wanted to die. I wanted to kill myself and just end everything because I felt that I was at the point of no return. My aunt was in somewhat of a shock because I had never expressed feelings of suicide, but she really just listened to me and gave me three words that saved my life. She said, "Call on Jesus."

Just those three words brought tears to my eyes. It was imperative that I needed to get myself together so I took her advice and cried out to God for Him to help me break free from that attachment. I was more sincere with God than I had ever been, in my praise, my worship and personal relationship with him

He focused my mind and brought back peace. I had to fast and pray for this breakthrough. He gave me the boldness and courage to fully walk away and leave it in the past. He showed me how I had so much more to do on this Earth. He opened my eyes of all the people that needed my testimony to help them break free. He showed me that I was alive because there was truly more to be done. It was not an easy process by far, but I learned about courage and integrity in a different way. Sometimes in life, we go through things that the devil throws at us that are meant to destroy us, but God will take situations the enemy meant for our bad and turn them around for our good. That makes it possible for us to be able to come out with our hands lifted up in praise and adoration.

Understand that people can carry spirits and demons that can be felt. Many times, God will send warnings to try to prevent close connections from these people if we aren't equipped to handle the situation. It is important to be careful of who you allow to come into your life—whether it be seasonal or not. Some people are just people that you are going to meet and go separate ways. When we try to force something that is supposed to repel against one another, God will sometimes throw His hands up and say, "I'm just going to let you do it your way."

Some learning experiences we go through in life can be avoided if we don't try to play "god" in our own lives. Trusting in God definitely plays an imperative role. Many of us are generally people who like to have control over pretty much everything in life. We don't like when we don't understand or know the answers to whatever problems are presented. It is when we lose control we worry and become stressed about various things instead of putting our trust in God. Faith coincides with trust. Having faith in God is truly believing as well as trusting in him and everything He has for us. Allow God to be who He is in your life and watch things change for the better. Allow yourself to be arrested in His love.

A HIGHER PURPOSE

FORGIVEN

Forgiveness was a thing I really struggled with for a long time. Truth be told, so many others struggle with it as well. Preachers and teachers are always telling us the importance of forgiveness, but what so many fail to tell us is *how* to forgive. I found that one of the main reasons why they don't touch on how to forgive is because it is different for all of us.

There is not a step-by-step guide how to forgive other than knowing that it takes God. In life, we all go through different experiences, which yield different effects and reactions. With that being said, some things are easier for one to forgive than others. I may struggle with forgiving someone who punched me while you may just turn the other cheek and keep it moving. Neither one of us would be wrong. We aren't wrong for having a long or short forgiveness process. However, I will tell you that once you begin the forgiveness process for whatever it is that has been holding you hostage, freedom will find you. It is in freedom that we are able to move forward in purpose. Until you are free from all that hold you back, you won't reach your full capacity.

The enemy will try to play both sides like you blaming yourself as well as being a victim. He will try to double whammy you, especially with things that transpire that are out of your control like sexual abuse or parental abandonment. He will attempt to haunt and taunt your mind with things of the past, which will then cause you to hold even more anger in your heart.

At the same time, he will begin to make you believe that you are the cause of what has happened. He'd want you to believe that you really played a part and something you did brought on what has transpired. The self-blame game is something that can really halt the process to true freedom. The enemy knows that if he can keep you bound then you won't be successful in walking further into purpose.

It is important that you know that you are not to blame for anything that has happened to you outside of your control. Knowing that through it all, God has not forgotten you. He is always standing by your side. Once you are able to move past self-blame, the enemy will then try other tactics. He will make you want to take things into your own hands. Some people want to get the individual who wronged them back and others wish the most horrible things over their lives. While it is okay to be hurt and upset, it is not okay to do wrong in return.

No matter what the reason behind the other party doing what they did, it will never be right to do it back. I get it: the natural reaction to anything that comes against you is to retaliate, but aren't you glad that God isn't like that? All the things we do as humans against the will of God and what is His response to us? Love, Grace, and Mercy.

Aside from that, God loves you so much that He made it so you don't have to get back at anyone. "Vengeance is mine," said the Lord. I have found him to be a God of Justice. He does not allow His children to be hurt and He not cover our backs. Some things you may see and other things you may not. God lets us know in his Word that He has us covered. Our God of Justice will get those who do His children harm. In the same manner, we should never rejoice due to our enemies' downfall. It could have been you in their shoes. You don't know what happened to cause them to be the way they are.

Not justifying what they did, but reminding you that even when they fall, they are still subject to grace and mercy. No matter how bad of a person they were, grace and mercy are still available to them just like salvation is available. God sent His son Jesus to die for those horrible parents, that child molester, that rapist, that manipulator, that thief, that murderer; the list of things goes on & on for the types of people he died for, and Jesus was crucified for all people and every sin attached to us. No one is disqualified from the benefits of God's wondrous grace because of our past, present, or even our future.

My favorite part of forgiveness is that it really isn't for the people who hurt you. It is really for you. It allows you to be free. Imagine you have hatred in your heart towards an ex-lover. In the moment when that lover became an ex, the hatred was born and it created an invisible carry-on bag of rocks. That's 25 pounds of rocks now attached to you plus the weight of the bag. Now you have a bag of hatred, then on top of that, another bag gets added on from pain from the mental abuse caused in your life. Now you have 50 pounds of extra weight on top of what you already have to carry. Your load just got two times heavier from holding on to the hatred and the pain instead of letting them go. Forgiveness is the ultimate key to letting go. In forgiving that ex-lover alone, the hatred and pain would be released. Can you imagine carrying 50 pounds of extra weight every single day? When the sun rises, it's with you and when it sets, it is still there.

I went around for years with extra weight and one day, I decided to choose me over them. My mental, physical, spiritual, and emotional health was not worth the things someone else caused me. I had to ask God to help me to forgive them, help me find love like He did for those who hurt Him and He is our Father. God wanted to offer a baggage claim for me, but I had to be willing to let it go. I released my baggage into His hands for Him to destroy and rid me of. I hated the way the baggage felt and even how it made me look. The heaviness caused me to look physically different.

So do whatever you have to do to break free and release the pain to God. If it takes going to the grave of that one who wronged you and telling them you forgive them—do it! Some may say that's too much, but they don't know what having that baggage has cost you.

Forget about what others would think about you forgiving someone. Don't allow opinions of others stop you from getting your freedom back. At some point in life, we must solely focus on ourselves. When it comes to forgiveness, it's okay be selfish, because it's for you. Let go and let God to come into your heart and help you forgive.

HEALED

I was finally a young man healed from the past. In finding out my purpose in life, I had to go through many trials and tests. I experienced various situations that caused so much damage and brokenness. So much pain and so many wounds were left open for years. I placed so many band-aids over them, trying to wrap up the pain. I never really treated the wounds before covering them up. You see, band-aids are only good when the wound has been treated. The sole purpose of the band-aid is to protect a wound that has been treated until it is healed.

So, when I was just trying to cover up the fact that I was hurt from being abandoned, I was really just prolonging the healing process. In order to be able to truly heal, we must not just try to patch things and keep it moving. We have to go through the process if we want to be free. To have freedom in every step we take in life is what we should strive for. The healing process to me is broken down into three impactful categories of life: acceptance, action, and healing.

In order for acceptance to be present, we have to accept the fact that we were wounded and knowing that it doesn't make you less than because of it. The next step of the process is action. If you want to be healed completely, we must take action. We have to go through proper treatment before the wound can be mended. No one's actions plan is alike and that is part of what makes us unique. For me, I took Christian psychotherapy and started to write music. Within that, forgiveness found its way through to my heart. Ultimately, it was God who was able to take His needle and sew up the wounds completely to the point where some don't even have any scars. Jehovah-Rapha is his name: "the God who heals." Now I am one that truly believes in therapy and counseling, but if God is not involved in the process, then we won't reach total healing. We can all agree and say it's nothing worse than when something is trying to heal, but sudden bumps or movements remind us of the pain and the fact that there is even a wound there in the first place. When total healing isn't reached, that four-letter word will haunt you and do everything it can to halt the healing process. The PAST: that thing will come after you whether you sent for it or not.

I call the last part of the process the healing portion. In this part of the process, it is where I found the past will really try to come in and make an appearance. It's in this moment when after we have taken the actions necessary for our healing process, our past will show its funky behind and will do everything to bring us down. It will try to remind us of who we were and used to be, and remind us of the traumatic things that transpired. The fight with the past can be the hardest part of the process because it knows exactly how to hold things over us. It knows the triggers and ways to get to our core.

The past doesn't come to play fair or follow any rules—so why should we? For this reason alone, we really need God, for He is our keeper, our stronger tower, our peacemaker, our healer, and most of all our Savior. He is no respect of person, so no matter who you are or what you have done he will offer healing and peace to you if you let him. Once you accept that healing needs to take place then action must be made in order to obtain the healing. Total healing from all things that have once bound you is the goal; 99 and a half just won't do—we want one-hundred percent healing.

While the healing process is not easy, with God, it is more than possible. He will comfort and keep you, no matter how small or large the wound. He can mend and restore all that was lost. He has shown me in so many ways that He really does care and He is sovereign. He doesn't want us to be bound and stuck. God wants us to take our tests and tell our testimonies. He wants us to overcome and share hope with others, because we overcome ourselves just by telling of His goodness.

Many times, God will allow us to go through just to see if He can trust us. Trust us to not forsake Him. Trust us to keep pushing and not giving up. Trust us with more. He wants to see how we will respond to the pressure. Often, before God gives us things, He will take us through a test to see if we can handle what is to come. Sometimes, it's not even about pass or fail, but more so about how we choose to go through. When you go through with God, you will always come out on top.

God has been with me on this journey of life. While on this journey, there has been a lot of laughs, tears, much joy, and strength that has been added to make me stronger than I ever knew I would be. Purpose is something that every single human has. Everything in this world has a purpose: from the rock to the eagle, from the snake to the tree, from the man to the woman, from me to you. Many of us have been called to a higher purpose that is greater than our being, greater than even our imagination could think.

God wants each of us to fulfill and walk in our purpose at the greatest capacity, which leads us to destiny.

Your destiny and purpose are both too important and vital to the world to give up. I don't care what you have been through; it was all a part of the shaping of you. It was a part of your purpose and that's something the enemy cannot take from you.

Remember when you are going through that it is possible that you are going through to help someone else down the line who will need your story. I did not always know my purpose. I was often looking in the wrong places for it to find me. All along, my purpose started with me: I had to do a self-evaluation in finding out who Javonté really was. It was when I found myself that purpose found me.

My purpose in life is quite simple: take the life experiences God has brought me through and share how He brought me out. My purpose is to inspire and pour into those who need that extra push. God created me to be a helper for others. It was not until I began to share what He had done for me, that things started to change for the better. God showed my why I exist and now it's time for you. I want you to dig deep and grab hold of yourself. Find out what it is that has given you cause to still be here. God has you here for a reason. It is for purpose, and once you discover your purpose, run in it. The saddest thing is when so many don't go after their destiny and die with unfulfilled purpose. Would you rather leave this world full of all the things that God planted in you to release or leave this world empty knowing that you had given all you could give?

A HIGHER PURPOSE

A Special Thanks

Thank you for purchasing my first book. It is my heart's desire that you enjoyed it and that you were encouraged while entertained. I hope that something in this book was a reminder that you have a purpose, and that there is a reason God allowed you to be here.

If you would like to connect with me, leave a review or keep up-to-date with events, please feel free to find and follow me on any of the Social Media listed below:

Facebook: Javonte M Wright

Twitter: @JavonteMWright

Instagram: @Javonte.W

Clubhouse: @Javonte.W

www.ingramcontent.com/pod-product-compliance
Lightning Source LLC
LaVergne TN
LVHW021600070426
835507LV00014B/1883